IT TAKES A LONG TIME TO BECOME **YOUNG**

WORDS TO GROW YOUNG BY

RICHARD KEHL

DARLING & COMPANY • MMVIII

FILE UNDER SELF-HELP

PRINTED IN CHINA THROUGH COLORCRAFT LTD., HONG KONG
ISBN13 978-1-59583-262-7

DARLING & COMPANY
A DIVISION OF LAUGHING ELEPHANT

WWW.LAUGHINGELEPHANT.COM

TABLE OF CONTENTS

IT TAKES A LONG TIME

TO BECOME YOUNG

LIVING

What is life? It is the flash of a firefly in the night. It is the breath of a buffalo in the wintertime. It is the little shadow which runs across the grass and loses itself in the sunset.

CROWFOOT, BLACKFOOT WARRIOR

To live is so startling, it leaves little room for other occupations.

EMILY DICKINSON

Would that life were like the shadow cast by a wall or a tree, but it is like the shadow of a bird in flight.

THE TALMUD

The bird doesn't sing because it has an answer, it sings because it has a song.

MAYA ANGELOU

How short life must be, if something so fragile can last a lifetime.

FRANZ KAFKA

And yet, is this not what life is? This is what I think: That the countless paltry, timid, petty, and shameful details ultimately still amount to a wonderful whole – a whole that would not exist if it depended upon us to understand it.

RAINER MARIA RILKE

IT TAKES A LONG TIME

Life is short, but it is wide.

SPANISH PROVERB

The truth is that life is delicious, horrible, charming, frightful, sweet, bitter, and that it is everything.

ANATOLE FRANCE

The meaning of life is that it stops.

FRANZ KAFKA

They say the movies should be more like life. I think life should be more like the movies.

MYRNA LOY

The extreme oddness of existence is what reconciles me to it.

LOGAN PEARSALL SMITH

Experience is the worst teacher: it gives the test before presenting the lesson.

VERNON LAW

Life is the art of drawing without an eraser.

JOHN GARDNER

To live is to be slowly born.

ANTOINE DE SAINT-EXUPERY

TO BECOME YOUNG

It is a funny thing about life, if you refuse to accept anything but the best, you very often get it: if you utterly decline to make do with what you get, then somehow or other you are very likely to get what you want.

W. SOMERSET MAUGHAM

I realized that I never had the least interest in living, but only in this which I am doing right now, something which is parallel to life, of it at the same time, and beyond it.

HENRY MILLER

Life is a horizontal fall.

JEAN COCTEAU

Life has been created quite truthfully in order to surprise us.

RAINER MARIA RILKE

Life is painting a picture, not doing a sum.

OLIVER WENDELL HOLMES, JR.

Dying is no accomplishment; we all do that. Living is the thing.

RED SMITH

Life is ours to be spent, not to be saved.

D.H. LAWRENCE

IT TAKES A LONG TIME

I love living, I have some problems with my life, but living is the best thing they've come up with so far.

NEIL SIMON

Don't tell me the plot ... I'm just a bit player.

RAYMOND CHANDLER

I have found that if you love life, life will love you back.

ARTHUR RUBINSTEIN

I believe in life after birth.

MAXIE DUNHAM

Life begins when a person first realizes how soon it ends.

MARCELENE COX

COURAGE

Be a ringing glass that shatters as it rings.

RAINER MARIA RILKE

What you risk reveals what you value.

JEANETTE WINTERSON

TO BECOME YOUNG

I postpone death by living, by suffering, by error, by risking, by giving, by losing.

ANAÏS NIN

And the trouble is, if you don't risk anything, you risk even more.

ERICA JONG

I just kept on doing what everyone starts out doing. The real question is, why did other people stop?

WILLIAM STAFFORD

If there is one door in the castle you have been told not to go through, you must. Otherwise, you'll just be rearranging furniture in rooms you've already been in.

ANNE LAMOTT

The problem is you. Bite on the nail ... swallow it and digest it, and get on with your life.

MARTHA GELLHORN

The only interesting answers are those which destroy the questions.

SUSAN SONTAG

Brave as a postage stamp crossing the ocean.

CHARLES SIMIC

IT TAKES A LONG TIME

Courage can't see around corners, but goes around them anyway.

MIGNON MCLAUGHLIN

What we truly and earnestly aspire to be, that in some sense we are. The mere aspiration, by changing the frame of the mind, for the moment realizes itself.

ANNA JAMESON

I am seeing so far tonight that I am blinded by the space between me and the inevitable.

HAZEL HALL

Perhaps all the dragons of our lives are princesses who are only waiting to see us once beautiful and brave.

RAINER MARIA RILKE

The one I will become will catch me.

J. CORCORAN

Risk! Risk anything! … Do the hardest thing on earth for you. Act for yourself. Face the truth.

KATHERINE MANSFIELD

Inside my empty bottle I was constructing a lighthouse while all the others were making ships.

CHARLES SIMIC

TO BECOME YOUNG

The champ may have lost his stuff temporarily or permanently, he can't be sure. When he can no longer throw his high hard one, he throws his heart instead. He throws something. He just doesn't walk off the mound and weep.

RAYMOND CHANDLER

Ultimately we know deeply that the other side of every fear is freedom.

MARILYN FERGUSON

There is not enough darkness in all the world to put out the light of even one small candle.

ROBERT ALDEN

I have not failed. I have successfully discovered twelve hundred ideas that don't work.

THOMAS EDISON

When I was thirteen, my father took me aside and told me that all a girl needed to know to get by in life was written on the top of a mayonnaise jar. I puzzled for days about the meaning of the phrase, "Refrigerate After Opening" – until my father remarked that in his day mayo jars always said, "Keep Cool, Don't Freeze."

C.E. CRIMMINS

A ship in harbor is safe, but that is not what ships are built for.

JOHN A. SHEDD

IT TAKES A LONG TIME

The unknown is what it is. And to be frightened of it is what sends everybody scurrying around chasing dreams, illusions, wars, peace, love, hate, all that … Accept that it's unknown and it's plain sailing.

JOHN LENNON

Piglet was so excited at the idea of being useful that he forgot to be frightened any more.

A.A. MILNE

CURIOSITY

There is one thing which gives radiance to everything. It is the idea of something around the corner.

G.K. CHESTERTON

To return to what exists to pure possibility; to reduce what is seen to pure visibility; that is the deep, the hidden work.

PAUL VALERY

A rock pile ceases to be a rock pile the moment a single man contemplates it, bearing within him the image of a cathedral.

ANTOINE DE SAINT-EXUPERY

Most new discoveries are suddenly-seen things that were always there.

SUSANNE K. LANGER

TO BECOME YOUNG

Nothing in the world can one imagine beforehand, not the least thing. Everything is made up of so many unique particulars that cannot be foreseen.

RAINER MARIA RILKE

What helps me go forward is that I stay receptive, I feel that anything can happen.

ANOUK AIMEE

One thing life taught me: if you are interested, you never have to look for new interests. They come to you. When you are genuinely interested in one thing, it will always lead to something else.

ELEANOR ROOSEVELT

The important thing is not to stop questioning. Curiosity has its own reason for existing. One cannot help but be in awe when he contemplates the mysteries of eternity, of life, of the marvelous structure of reality. It is enough if one tries merely to comprehend a little of this mystery everyday. Never lose a holy curiosity.

ALBERT EINSTEIN

My favorite thing is to go where I have never gone.

DIANE ARBUS

IT TAKES A LONG TIME

POSITIVE ATTITUDE

Since we are destined to live out our lives in the prison of our minds, our one duty is to furnish it well.

PETER USTINOV

I am the circumstance.

OCTAVIO PAZ

Luck is believing you're lucky.

TENNESSEE WILLIAMS

I think of life itself, now, as a wonderful play that I've written for myself … And so my purpose is to have the most fun playing my part.

SHIRLEY MACLAINE

Life is 10 percent what you make it, and 90 percent how you take it.

IRVING BERLIN

I always say to myself, what is the most important thing we can think about at this extraordinary moment.

FRANÇOIS DE LA ROCHEFOUCAULD

I invented my life by taking for granted that everything I did not like would have an opposite, which I would like.

COCO CHANEL

TO BECOME YOUNG

There is a fountain of youth: it is your mind, your talents, the creativity you bring to your life and the lives of people you love. When you learn to tap this source, you will have truly defeated age.

SOPHIA LOREN

I am happy and content because I think I am.

ALAIN-RENE LESAGE

A mistake is simply another way of doing things.

KATHARINE GRAHAM

You live with your thoughts – so be careful what they are.

EVA ARRINGTON

If your daily life seems poor, do not blame it; blame yourself, tell yourself that you are not poet enough to call forth its riches.

RAINER MARIA RILKE

I believe fervently in our species and have no patience with the current fashion of running down the human being. On the contrary, we are a spectacular, splendid manifestation of life. We matter. We are the newest, youngest, brightest things around.

LEWIS THOMAS

I have woven a parachute of everything broken.

WILLIAM STAFFORD

IT TAKES A LONG TIME

If, every day, I dare to remember that I am here on loan, that this house, this hillside, these minutes are all leased to me, not given, I will never despair.

ERICA JONG

The question is how immediately are you going to say yes to no matter what unpredictability.

JOHN CAGE

To all that has run its course, and to the vast unsayable number of beings abounding in Nature, add yourself gladly, and cancel the cost.

RAINER MARIA RILKE

You have to act as if. That's a big recovery item: act as if. Act as if you believe.

ELIZABETH WURTZEL

What can anyone give you greater than now, starting here, right in this room, when you turn around?

WILLIAM STAFFORD

We find what we search for — or, if we don't find it, we become it.

JESSAMYN WEST

Be a lamp, or a lifeboat, or a ladder.

RUMI

TO BECOME YOUNG

Never let your head hang down. Never give up and sit down and grieve. Find another way. And don't pray when it rains if you don't pray when the sun shines.

SATCHEL PAIGE

It is a great piece of skill to know how to guide your luck even while waiting for it.

BALTASAR GRACIÁN

Success is aiming for the stars, because if you fall short, you are going to land on the moon, and there are not too many people on the moon now, are there?

AMY VAN DYKEN, OLYMPIC GOLD MEDALIST

You must learn day by day, year by year, to broaden your horizon. The more things you love, the more you are interested in, the more you enjoy, the more you are indignant about – the more you have left when anything happens.

ETHEL BARRYMORE

I used to be addicted to overcoming things. Now, my goal is to get out of my own way.

SHIRLEY MACLAINE

I imagine that yes is the only living thing.

E.E. CUMMINGS

IT TAKES A LONG TIME

It is never too late to be what you might have been.

GEORGE ELIOT

When I was born and where and how I have lived is unimportant. It is what I have done with where I have been that should be of interest.

GEORGIA O'KEEFFE

People are always blaming their circumstances for what they are. I don't believe in circumstances. The people who get on in this world are the people who get up and look for the circumstances they want, and, if they can't find them, make them.

GEORGE BERNARD SHAW

I'll just hit the dry side of the ball.

STAN MUSIAL, ON HOW TO HANDLE A SPITBALL

Whenever you fall, pick something up.

OSWALD AVERY

If the sky falls, hold up your hands.

SPANISH PROVERB

The secret of life is to have a task, something you devote your entire life to, something you bring everything to, every minute of the day for the rest of your life and the most important thing is, it must be something you cannot possibly do.

HENRY MOORE

TO BECOME YOUNG

I think I can. I think I can. I think I can.
I thought I could. I thought I could. I thought I could.

MABEL BRAGG

Every wall is a door.

RALPH WALDO EMERSON

Believe that life is worth living and your belief will help create the fact.

WILLIAM JAMES

Remember, life is not what happens to you but what you make of what happens to you. Everyone dies, but not everyone fully lives. Too may people are having "near-life experiences."

ANONYMOUS.

I am not a has-been. I am a will-be.

LAUREN BACALL

I always admired Chekhov for building a new house when he was dying of tuberculosis.

LEON EDEL

IT TAKES A LONG TIME

DO IT NOW

You decide you'll wait for your pitch. Then as the ball starts toward the plate, you think about your stance. And then you think about your swing. And then you realize that the ball that went past you for a strike was your pitch.

BOBBY MURCER

The word "now" is like a bomb through the window, and it ticks.

ARTHUR MILLER

Why not seize the pleasure at once? How often is happiness destroyed by preparation, foolish preparation?

JANE AUSTEN

Don't even make a list. Do everything right now.

SIGOURNEY WEAVER

Unless a man has trained himself for his chance, the chance will only make him ridiculous.

W. MATTHEWS

What isn't tried won't work.

CLAUDE MCDONALD

TO BECOME YOUNG

The way to achieve a difficult thing is to set it in motion.

KATE O'BRIEN

People permit life to slide past them like a deft pickpocket, their purse
—not yet missed and now too late—in his hand.

EDNA FERBER

Today.

WORD CARVED ON A STONE ON JOHN RUSKIN'S DESK

Procrastination – the art of keeping up with yesterday.

DON MARQUIS

Everyone lets the present moment slip by, and then looks for it as
though it were somewhere else.

HAGAKURE

Spend the afternoon. You can't take it with you.

ANNIE DILLARD

We cannot put off living until we are ready. The most salient charac-
teristic of life is its coerciveness: it is always urgent, "here and now"
without any possible postponement. Life is fired at us point blank.

JOSE ORTEGA Y GASSET

IT TAKES A LONG TIME

Tomorrow's life is too late. Live Today.

MARCUS VALERIUS MARTIALIS

I have always known that at last I would take this road, but yesterday I did not know that it would be today.

NARIHARA

We have only this moment, sparkling like a star in our hand ... and melting like a snowflake. Let us use it before it is too late.

MARIE BEYON RAY

You don't need endless time and perfect conditions. Do it now. Do it today. Do it for twenty minutes and watch your heart start beating.

BARBARA SHER

You cannot do a kindness too soon, for you never know how soon it will be too late.

RALPH WALDO EMERSON

Never put off until tomorrow what you can do today, because if you enjoy it today, you can do it again tomorrow.

ANONYMOUS

Twenty years from now you will be more disappointed by the things you didn't do than the ones you did. Sail away from the safe harbor. Dream. Discover.

MARK TWAIN

TO BECOME YOUNG

CHANGE

Let's waltz the rumba.

FATS WALLER

I can't understand why people are frightened of new ideas. I'm frightened of the old ones.

JOHN CAGE

When I let go of what I am, I become what I might be.

LAO TZU

If everything is under control, you are going too slow.

MARIO ANDRETTI

If you do nothing unexpected, nothing unexpected happens.

FAY WELDON

The arrow endures the string, and in the gathering momentum becomes more than itself. Because to stay is to be nowhere.

RAINER MARIA RILKE

Life is change. Growth is optional. Choose Wisely.

KAREN KAISER CLARK

IT TAKES A LONG TIME

To correct: to arrange surprise.

R. BUCKMINSTER FULLER

The greatest and most important problems of life are all in a certain sense insoluble. They can never be solved, but only outgrown.

CARL JUNG

We must be willing to get rid of the life we've planned, so as to have the life that is waiting for us.

JOSEPH CAMPBELL

"How does one become a butterfly?" she asked pensively. "You must want to fly so much that you are willing to give up being a caterpillar."

TRINA PAULUS

When you're stuck in a spiral, to change all aspects of the spin you need only to change one thing.

CHRISTINA BALDWIN

If you can't change your fate, change your attitude.

AMY TAN

Forgiveness is a way that we can alter the past.

DAVID BELLA

TO BECOME YOUNG

We cannot change anything unless we accept it.

CARL JUNG

Go and wake up your luck.

PERSIAN PROVERB

I have a theory that every time you make an important choice, the part of you left behind continues the other life you could have had.

JEANETTE WINTERSON

Transform? Yes, for it is our task to impress this provisional, transient earth upon ourselves so deeply, so agonizingly, and so passionately that its essence rises up again "invisibly" within us.

RAINER MARIA RILKE

Unless one says goodbye to what one loves, and unless one travels to completely new territories, one can expect merely a long wearing away of oneself and an eventual extinction.

JEAN DUBUFFET

To change skins, evolve into new cycles, I feel one has to learn to discard. If one changes internally, one should not continue to live with the same objects.

ANAÏS NIN

It is never too late – in fiction or in life – to revise.

NANCY THAYER

IT TAKES A LONG TIME

The need for change bulldozed a road down the center of my mind.

MAYA ANGELOU

The moment of change is the only poem.

ADRIENNE RICH

This, then is IT; not the crude anguish of physical death, but the incomparable pangs of the mysterious mental maneuver needed to pass from one state of being to another. Easy, you know, does it, son.

VLADIMIR NABOKOV

Keep doing what you're doing and you'll keep getting what you're getting.

ANONYMOUS

The best way to make your dreams come true is to wake up.

PAUL VALERY

In spite of illness, in spite of the archenemy sorrow, one can remain alive long past the usual date of disintegration if one is unafraid of change, insatiable in intellectual curiosity, interested in big things, and happy in small ways.

EDITH WHARTON

When you arrive at a fork in the road, take it.

YOGI BERRA

TO BECOME YOUNG

All changes, even the most longed for, have their melancholy; for what we leave behind us is a part of ourselves; we must die to one life before we can enter another.

ANATOLE FRANCE

If we could see the miracle of a single flower clearly, our whole life would change.

BUDDHA

Even if you're on the right track, you'll get run over if you just sit there.

WILL ROGERS

You can't turn back the clock. But you can wind it up again.

BONNIE PRUDDEN

At fifty, the madwoman in the attic breaks loose, stomps down the stairs, and sets fire to the house. She won't be imprisoned anymore.

ERICA JONG

Whenever I draw a circle, I immediately want to step out of it.

R. BUCKMINSTER FULLER

The world is quite right. It does not have to be consistent.

CHARLOTTE PERKINS GILLMAN

IT TAKES A LONG TIME

There is a time for departure even when there's no certain place to go.

TENNESSEE WILLIAMS

The first problem for all of us, men and women, is not to learn, but to unlearn.

GLORIA STEINEM

FEAR

Here is the time for telling. Speak and make known: More and more the things we could experience are lost to us, banished by our failure to imagine them.

RAINER MARIA RILKE

I've been absolutely terrified every moment of my life and I've never let it keep me from doing a single thing I wanted to do.

GEORGIA O'KEEFFE

I have not ceased being fearful, but I have ceased to let fear control me. I have accepted fear as a part of life, specifically the fear of change, the fear of the unknown, and I have gone ahead despite the pounding in the heart that says: turn back, turn back, you'll die if you venture too far.

ERICA JONG

TO BECOME YOUNG

One of the reasons mature people stop learning is that they become less and less willing to risk failure.

JOHN W. GARDNER

I wanted to be scared again … I wanted to feel unsure again. That's the only way I learn, the only way I feel challenged.

CONNIE CHUNG

Don't be afraid your life will end; be afraid it will never begin.

GRACE HANSEN

How many pessimists end up by desiring the things they fear, in order to prove they are right?

ROBERT MALLET

HAPPINESS

Happiness will never be any greater than the idea we have of it.

MAURICE MAETERLINCK

I'm happier … I guess I made up my mind to be that way.

MERLE HAGGARD

IT TAKES A LONG TIME

Remember that happiness is a way of travel – not a destination.

ROY M. GOODMAN

I am so rich that I must give myself away.

EGON SCHIELE

My life has no purpose, no direction, no aim, no meaning, and yet I'm happy. I can't figure it out. What am I doing right?

CHARLES SCHULZ

Be patient toward all that is unsolved in your heart and try to love the questions themselves. Do not seek the answers, which cannot be given you because you would not be able to live them. And the point is, to live everything. Live the questions now. Perhaps you will then gradually, without noticing it, live along some distant day into the answer.

RAINER MARIA RILKE

There are two things to aim at in life: first, to get what you want; and, after that, to enjoy it. Only the wisest of mankind achieve the second.

LOGAN PEARSALL SMITH

I am a kind of paranoiac in reverse. I suspect people of plotting to make me happy.

J.D. SALINGER

TO BECOME YOUNG

Nothing is more fatal to happiness than the remembrance of happiness.

ANDRE GIDE

For what end is served by all the expenditure of suns and planets and moons, of stars and Milky Ways, of comets and nebula, of worlds evolving and passing away, if at last a happy man does not involuntarily rejoice in his existence?

FRIEDRICH NIETZSCHE

Happiness makes up in height for what it lacks in length.

ROBERT FROST

My advice to you is not to inquire why or whither, but just enjoy your ice cream while it's on your plate.

THORNTON WILDER

Too much of a good thing can be wonderful.

MAE WEST

You just can't complain about being alive. It's self-indulgent to be unhappy.

GENA ROWLANDS

We must select the illusion which appeals to our temperament, and embrace it with passion if we want to be happy.

CYRIL CONNOLLY

IT TAKES A LONG TIME

As I grow more to understand life less and less, I learn to live it more and more.

JULES RENARD

It is only possible to live happily ever after on a day-to-day basis.

MARGARET BONANNO

Follow your bliss.

JOSEPH CAMPBELL

A little unlearning goes a long way.

ANONYMOUS

BELIEF

Many a time I have wanted to stop talking and find out what I really believed.

WALTER LIPPMANN

If you think you can, you can. And if you think you can't, you're right.

MARY KAY ASH

Truth is simply whatever you can bring yourself to believe.

ALICE CHILDRESS

TO BECOME YOUNG

We believe as much as we can. We would believe everything if we could.

WILLIAM JAMES

I make the most of all that comes and the least of all that goes.

SARA TEASDALE

Sometimes I have believed as many as six impossible things before breakfast.

LEWIS CARROLL

A man has made at least a start on discovering the meaning of a human life when he plants shade trees under which he knows full well he will never sit.

D. ELTON TRUEBLOOD

Among all my patients in the second half of life...there has not been one whose problem in the last resort was not that of finding a religious outlook on life.

CARL JUNG

If one asks for success and prepares for failure, he will get the situation he has prepared for.

FLORENCE SCOVEL SHINN

IT TAKES A LONG TIME

I don't know whether this world has a meaning that transcends it. But I know that I do not know that meaning and it is impossible for me to know.

ALBERT CAMUS

WONDER

We carry within us the wonders we seek without us.

SIR THOMAS BROWNE

The brain is wider than the sky.

EMILY DICKINSON

Life is not made of the number of breaths we take, but of the moments that take our breath away.

ANONYMOUS

To be alive, to be able to see, to walk – it's all a miracle. I have adopted the technique of living life from miracle to miracle.

ARTHUR RUBINSTEIN

I remember the day when I learned to whistle. It was in spring and new sounds were all around.

GORDON LEA, AGE 11

TO BECOME YOUNG

Good-bye world ... Good-bye to clocks ticking ... and Mama's sun-flowers. And food and coffee. And new-ironed dresses and hot baths ... and sleeping and waking up. Oh, earth, you're too wonderful for anybody to realize you.

THORNTON WILDER

INDIVIDUALITY

Be yourself. Who else is better qualified?

FRANK J. BIGLIN II

I do not create myself, I choose myself.

SÖREN KIERKEGAARD

If I am not for myself, then who will be for me? If I am not for others, who am I for? And if not now, when?

TALMUD

To succeed, consider what is as though it were past. Deem yourself inevitable and take credit for it. If you find you no longer believe, enlarge the temple

W.S. MERWIN

IT TAKES A LONG TIME

I owe my success to having listened respectfully to the very best advice, and then going away and doing the exact opposite.

G.K. CHESTERTON

If you always do what pleases you, at least one person is pleased.

KATHARINE HEPBURN

How many cares one loses when one decides not to be something, but to be someone.

COCO CHANEL

It is the night again around me; I feel as though there had been lightning – for a brief span of time I was entirely in my element and in my light.

FRIEDRICH NIETZSCHE

Cherish forever what makes you unique, 'cuz you're really a yawn if it goes!

BETTE MIDLER

Don't compromise yourself. You are all you've got.

JANIS JOPLIN

We must believe in free will, we have no choice.

ISAAC BASHEVIS SINGER

TO BECOME YOUNG

If you are not your own agent, you are some one else's.

ALICE MOLLOY

If you don't run your own life, someone else will.

JOHN ATKINSON

Be a pianist, not a piano.

A.R. ORAGE

I read and walked for miles at night along the beach, writing bad blank verse and searching endlessly for someone wonderful who would step out of the darkness and change my life. It never crossed my mind that person could be me.

ANNA QUINDLEN

I don't want to be a passenger in my own life.

DIANE ACKERMAN

Nobody can be exactly like me. Sometimes even I have trouble doing it.

TALLULAH BANKHEAD

When you turn the corner and run into yourself, then you know that you have turned all the corners that are left.

LANGSTON HUGHES

IT TAKES A LONG TIME

But if you travel far enough, one day you will recognize yourself coming down the road to meet yourself. And you will say Yes.

UNKNOWN

You are all you will ever have for certain.

JUNE HAVOC

Be faithful to that which exists nowhere but in yourself – and thus make yourself indispensable.

ANDRÉ GIDE.

The bad news is time flies. The good news is you're the pilot.

MICHAEL ALTSHULER

Success follows doing what you want to do! There is no other way to be successful.

MALCOLM FORBES

RESPONSIBILITY

I must be used, built into the solid fabric of life as far as there is any usable brick in me, and thrown aside when I am used up. It is only when I am being used that I can feel my own existence, enjoy my own life.

GEORGE BERNARD SHAW

TO BECOME YOUNG

We are taught you must blame your father, your sisters, your brothers, the school, the teachers – you can blame anyone, but never blame yourself. It's never your fault. But it's always your fault, because if you want to change, you're the one who has got to change. It's as simple as that, isn't it?

KATHARINE HEPBURN

You can't hope to be lucky. You have to prepare to be lucky.

TIMOTHY DOWD

Take your life in your own hands and what happens? A terrible thing. No one to blame.

ERICA JONG

I learn by going where I have to go.

THEODORE ROETHKE

It's a sad day when you find out that it's not accident or time or fortune but just yourself that kept things from you.

LILLIAN HELLMAN

It's only when we truly know and understand that we have a limited time on earth—and that we have no way of knowing when our time is up—that we will begin to live each day to the fullest, as if it was the only one we had.

ELISABETH KUBLER-ROSS

IT TAKES A LONG TIME

Only the dreamer can change the dream.

JOHN LOGAN

It's when you stop doing the stuff you have to make excuses for and when you stop making excuses for the stuff you have to do.

MARILYN VOS SAVANT

When you die God will hold you accountable for all the pleasures you were allowed in life that you denied yourself.

ANONYMOUS

You have more freedom than you are using.

DAN ATTOE

INVOLVEMENT

Do every act of your life as if it were your last.

MARCUS AURELIUS

How many times have you tried to shield yourself by reading the news-paper, watching television, or just spacing out? That is the $64,000 question: how much have you connected with yourself at all in your whole life?

CHÖGYAM TRUNGPA

TO BECOME YOUNG

Take the time to come home to yourself everyday.

ROBIN CASARJEAN

Is not life a hundred times too short for us to bore ourselves?

FRIEDRICH NIETZSCHE

The harder you work, the luckier you get.

GARY PLAYER

Concentration is everything. On the day I'm performing, I don't hear anything anyone else says to me.

LUCIANO PAVAROTTI

Being bored is an insult to oneself.

JULES RENARD

Look, I don't want to wax philosophic, but I will say that if you're alive you've got to flap your arms and legs, you've got to jump around a lot, for life is the very opposite of death, and therefore you must at the very least think noisy and colorfully, or you're not alive.

MEL BROOKS

One disadvantage of having nothing to do is you can't stop and rest.

FRANKLIN P. JONES

IT TAKES A LONG TIME

I don't want to get to the end of my life and find that I have lived just the length of it. I want to have lived the width of it, as well.

DIANE ACKERMAN

DIFFICULTIES

I try to take one day at a time, but sometimes several days attack me at once.

ASHLEIGH BRILLIANT

Sighing was, he believed, simply the act of taking in more oxygen to help the brain cope with an unusual or difficult set of circumstances.

MARGARET MILLER

Now for some heart work.

RAINER MARIA RILKE

We have no reason to mistrust our world, for it is not against us. Has it terrors, they are our terrors; has it abysses, those abysses belong to us: are dangers at hand, we must try to love them. And if only we arrange our life according to that principle which counsels us that we must always hold to the difficult, then that which now still seems to us the most alien will become what we most trust and find most faithful.

RAINER MARIA RILKE

TO BECOME YOUNG

When it is dark enough, you can see the stars.

CHARLES BEARD

We must endure our thoughts all night, until the bright obvious stands motionless in the cold.

WALLACE STEVENS

On some hill of despair the bonfire you kindle can light the great sky – though it's true, of course, to make it burn you have to throw yourself in.

GALWAY KINNELL

Yard by yard, it's very hard. But inch by inch, it's a cinch.

ANONYMOUS

And you do actually want to live? Then you are mistaken in calling it your duty to take on difficulties. So what is duty, then? It is a duty to love what is difficult … You have to be there when it needs you.

RAINER MARIA RILKE

I like living. I have sometimes been wildly, despairingly, acutely miserable, racked with sorrow, but through it all I still know quite certainly that just to be alive is a grand thing.

AGATHA CHRISTIE

Disappointments should be cremated, not embalmed.

HENRY S. HASKINS

IT TAKES A LONG TIME

If your house is on fire, warm yourself by it.

SPANISH PROVERB

… you will grow if you are sick in pain, experience losses, and if you do not put your head in the sand but take the pain and learn to accept it, not as a curse or punishment but as a gift to you with a very, very specific purpose.

ELISABETH KUBLER-ROSS

Nobody can make you feel inferior without your consent.

ELEANOR ROOSEVELT

Birds sing after a storm; why shouldn't people feel as free to delight in whatever remains to them?

ROSE KENNEDY

People fail forward to success.

MARY KAY ASH

They say that nobody is perfect. Then they tell you practice makes perfect. I wish they'd make up their minds.

WILT CHAMBERLAIN

On the door to success it says: push and pull.

YIDDISH PROVERB

TO BECOME YOUNG

You've got to be very careful if you don't know where you are going, because you might not get there.

YOGI BERRA

The Old Man of the Earth stooped over the floor of the cave, raised a huge stone from it, and left it leaning. It disclosed a great hole that went plumb-down. "That is the way," he said. "But there are no stairs," "You must throw yourself in. There is no other way."

GEORGE MACDONALD

OLD

How old would you be if you didn't know how old you are?

SATCHEL PAIGE

Her grandmother, as she gets older, is not fading but rather becoming more concentrated.

PAULETTE BATES ALDEN

Growing old is no more than a bad habit that a busy person has no time to form.

ANDRÉ MAUROIS

Age is mind over matter. If you don't mind, it doesn't matter.

SATCHEL PAIGE

IT TAKES A LONG TIME

Another belief of mine: that everyone else my age is an adult, whereas I am merely in disguise.

MARGARET ATWOOD

If you don't want to get old, don't mellow.

LINDA ELLERBEE

Just remember, once you're over the hill, you begin to pick up speed.

CHARLES SCHULZ

Those who love deeply never grow old; they may die of old age, but they die young.

ARTHUR WING PINERO

None are so old as those who have outlived enthusiasm.

HENRY DAVID THOREAU

Old age is that night of life, as night is the old age of day. Still, night is full of magnificence and, for many, it is more brilliant than the day.

ANNE-SOPHIE SWETCHINE

Age puzzles me. I thought it was a quiet time. My seventies were interesting and fairly serene, but my eighties are passionate. I grow more intense as I age.

FLORIDA SCOTT-MAXWELL

TO BECOME YOUNG

Age does not protect you from love, but love to some extent protects you from age.

JEANNE MOREAU

I am long on ideas, but short on time. I expect to live to be only about a hundred.

THOMAS ALVA EDISON

I believe in old age; to work and to grow old: this is what life expects of us. And then one day to be old and still be quite far from understanding everything – no, but to begin, but to love, but to suspect, but to be connected to what is remote and inexpressible, all the way up into the stars.

RAINER MARIA RILKE

Age is something that doesn't matter, unless you are a cheese.

BILLIE BURKE

If you prepare for old age, old age comes sooner.

ANONYMOUS

One part of him is old and another is still unborn.

ELIAS CANETTI

The great thing about getting older is that you don't lose all the other ages you've been.

MADELEINE L'ENGLE

IT TAKES A LONG TIME

I never feel age... If you have creative work you don't have age or time.

LOUISE NEVELSON

There is no old age. There is, as there always was, just you.

CAROL MATTHAU

We who are old know that age is more than a disability. It is an intense and varied experience, almost beyond our capacity at times, but something to be carried high.

FLORIDA SCOTT-MAXWELL

If I'd known I was gonna live this long, I'd have taken better care of myself.

UBIE BLAKE, AT 100 YEARS OF AGE

I was asked the other day: "What are you doing nowadays?" "I'm busy growing older," I answered, "It's a full-time job."

PAUL LEAUTAUD

Young. Old. Just words.

GEORGE BURNS (AT AGE 84)

I am luminous with age.

MERIDEL LE SUEUR

TO BECOME YOUNG

Age is not all decay; it is the ripening, the swelling of the fresh life within, that withers and bursts the husk.

GEORGE MACDONALD

YOUNG

It takes a long time to become young.

PABLO PICASSO

The idea is to die young as late as possible.

ASHLEY MONTAGUE

You are younger today than you ever will be again. Make use of it for the sake of tomorrow.

ANONYMOUS

To be seventy years young is sometimes far more cheerful and hopeful than to be forty years old.

OLIVER WENDELL HOLMES, JR.

We turn not older with years, but newer every day.

EMILY DICKINSON

IT TAKES A LONG TIME

Youth is something very new: twenty years ago no one mentioned it.

COCO CHANEL

You're never too old to become younger.

MAE WEST

I can remember, at the age of five, being told that childhood was the happiest period of life. I wept inconsolably, wished I were dead, and wondered how I should endure the boredom of the years to come.

BERTRAND RUSSELL

When it comes to staying young, a mind-lift beats a face-lift any day.

MARTY BUCELLA

It is an illusion that youth is happy, an illusion of those who have lost it.

SOMERSET MAUGHAM

I am much younger now than I was at twelve or anyway, less burdened.

FLANNERY O'CONNOR

I shall die very young … maybe seventy, maybe eighty, maybe ninety. But I shall be very young.

JEANNE MOREAU

TO BECOME YOUNG

NUMBERS

Twenty-three is said to be the prime of life by those who have reached so far and no farther. It shares this distinction with every age, from ten to three-score and ten.

STELLA BENSON

I've always roared with laughter when they say life begins at forty. That's the funniest remark ever. The day I was born was when life began for me.

BETTE DAVIS

It was only in my forties that I started feeling young.

HENRY MILLER

To me, old age is always fifteen years older than I am.

BARNARD M. BARUCH

I am just turning 40 and taking my time about it.

HAROLD LLOYD (IN HIS 70'S)

A man ninety years old was asked to what he attributed his longevity. "I reckon," he said, "it's because most nights I went to bed and slept when I should have sat up and worried."

DOROTHEA KENT

IT TAKES A LONG TIME

I refuse to admit that I'm more than fifty-two even if that does make my sons illegitimate.

LADY ASTOR

I'm sixty-three and I guess that puts me in with the geriatrics, but if there were fifteen months in every year, I'd be only forty-three.

JAMES THURBER

When you come to write my epitaph, Charles, let it be in these delicious words, "She had a long twenty-nine."

JAMES BARRIE

I'll never make the mistake of bein' seventy again.

CASEY STENGEL

Many people's tombstones should read, "Died at 30. Buried at 60."

NICHOLAS MURRAY BUTLER

In July, when I bury my nose in a hazel bush, I feel fifteen years old again. It's good! It smells of love!

JEAN-BAPTISTE-CAMILLE COROT

Life would be infinitely happier if we could only be born at the age of eighty and gradually approach eighteen.

MARK TWAIN

TO BECOME YOUNG

I am just an ingénue – and shall be till I'm 82.

NOEL COWARD

Some people die at 25 and aren't buried until they are 75.

BENJAMIN FRANKLIN

Oh to be seventy again.

OLIVER WENDELL HOLMES, JR.
(UPON SEEING AN ATTRACTIVE WOMAN ON HIS NINETIETH BIRTHDAY)

DEATH

Death is not the greatest loss in life. The greatest loss is what dies inside us while we live.

NORMAN COUSINS

The only thing you have to do is be born and live. Everything else is choice. And the sooner you learn it, the better your choices are.

JOLLY BUTLER

I warn you, I am living for the last time.

ANNA AKHMATOVA

IT TAKES A LONG TIME

Do not take life too seriously – you will never get out of it alive.

ELBERT HUBBARD

If you want to die happily, learn to live; if you would live happily, learn to die.

CELIO CALCAGNINI

The partition separating life from death is so tenuous. The unbeliev-able fragility of our organism suggests a vision on a screen: a kind of mist condenses itself into a human shape, lasts a moment and scatters.

CZESLAW MILOSZ

In the night of death, hope sees a star, and listening, love can hear the rustle of a wing.

ROBERT G. INGERSOLL

Those who welcome death have only tried it from the ears up.

WILSON MIZNER

There is no cure for birth and death save to enjoy the interval.

GEORGE SANTAYANA

TO BECOME YOUNG

LIVING IN THE PRESENT

Right now a moment of time is passing by!... We must become that moment.

PAUL CEZANNE

I am in the present. I cannot know what tomorrow will bring forth. I can only know what the truth is for me today. That is what I am called upon to serve, and I serve it in all lucidity.

IGOR STRAVINSKY

This – the immediate, everyday, and present experience – is IT, the entire and ultimate point for the existence of a universe.

ALAN WATTS

We aren't worried about posterity; we want it to sound good right now.

ANONYMOUS

It is so hard for us little human beings to accept this deal that we get. It's really crazy, isn't it? We get to live, then we have to die. What we put into every moment is all we have.

GILDA RADNER

Be always resolute with the present hour. Every moment is of infinite value.

GOETHE

IT TAKES A LONG TIME

When something does not insist on being noticed, when we aren't grabbed by the collar or struck on the skull by a presence or an event, we take for granted the very things that most deserve our gratitude.

CYNTHIA OZICK

Luck is largely a matter of paying attention.

SUSAN M. DOWD

There is one thing we can do, and the happiest people are those who do it to the limit of their ability. We can be completely present. We can be all here. We can give all our attention to the opportunity before us.

MARK VAN DOREN

I think the one lesson I have learned is that there is no substitute for paying attention.

DIANE SAWYER

Every day is a gift, which is why we call it the present.

ALFRED HITCHCOCK

Each experience has its own velocity according to which it wants to be lived if it is to be new, profound, and fruitful. To have wisdom means to discover this velocity in each individual case.

RAINER MARIA RILKE

TO BECOME YOUNG

FUTURE

Wishes are the memories coming from our future!

RAINER MARIA RILKE

The world is mine because it is haunted by possibilities.

JEAN-PAUL SARTRE

Light tomorrow with today.

ELIZABETH BARRETT BROWNING

I am my possibilities.

GABRIEL MARCEL

But to look back all the time is boring. Excitement lies in tomorrow.

NATALIA MAKAROVA

One ought to turn the most extreme possibility inside oneself into the measure for one's life, for our life is vast and can accommodate as much future as we are able to carry.

RAINER MARIA RILKE

It is the business of the future to be dangerous.

ALFRED NORTH WHITEHEAD

IT TAKES A LONG TIME

I began then to think of time as having a shape, something you could see, like a series of liquid transparencies, one laid on top of another. You don't look back along time but down through it, like water. Sometimes this comes to the surface, sometimes that, sometimes nothing. Nothing goes away.

MARGARET ATWOOD

Real generosity toward the future lies in giving all to the present.

ALBERT CAMUS

The afternoon knows what the morning never suspected.

SWEDISH PROVERB

We are the echo of the future.

W.S. MERWIN

Life is a series of collisions with the future; it is not the sum of what we have been, but what we yearn to be.

JOSE ORTEGA Y GASSET

There is no justification for present existence other than its expansion into an indefinitely open future.

SIMONE DE BEAUVOIR

TO BECOME YOUNG

STARTING OVER

If I had my life to live over again … I would have more actual troubles and less imaginary ones. Oh, I've had my moments, and if I had to do it over again, I'd have more of them. In fact, I'd try to have nothing else, just moments, one after another.

NADINE STAIR

If I had my life to live over again, I would start barefoot earlier in the spring.

85 YEAR OLD WOMAN

If I had to live my life again, I'd make all the same mistakes – only sooner.

TALLULAH BANKHEAD

DESIRE

Never let go of that fiery sadness called desire.

PATTI SMITH

I'll always push the envelope. To me, the ultimate sin in life is to be boring. I don't play it safe.

CYBIL SHEPHERD

55

IT TAKES A LONG TIME

I am a restlessness inside a stillness inside a restlessness.

DODIE SMITH

In purely spiritual matters, God grants all desires. Those who have less have asked for less.

SIMONE WEIL

Put your ear down close to your soul and listen hard.

ANNE SEXTON

I know that nothing has ever been real without my beholding it. All becoming has needed me. My looking ripens things, and they come toward me, to meet and be met.

RAINER MARIA RILKE

When you do something, you should burn yourself completely, like a good bonfire, leaving no trace of yourself.

SHUNKYU SUZUKI

But my soul is a fire that suffers if it doesn't burn. I need three or four cubic feet of new ideas every day, as a steamboat needs coal.

JEAN PREVOST

He felt a feather grow on every feather.

RAINER MARIA RILKE

TO BECOME YOUNG

You can have anything you want if you want it desperately enough. You must want it with an inner exuberance that erupts through the skin and joins the energy that created the world.

SHEILA GRAHAM

YOUTHFUL ATTITUDE

Dare to be naïve.

R. BUCKMINSTER FULLER

I never did a day's work in my life. It was all fun.

THOMAS EDISON

I have enjoyed greatly the second blooming that comes when you suddenly find – at the age of fifty, say – that a whole new life has opened before you, filled with things you can think about, study, or read about ... It is as if a fresh sap of ideas and thoughts was rising in you.

AGATHA CHRISTIE

The fresh start is always an illusion but a necessary one.

ELEANOR CLARK

Everyone is the age of their heart.

GUATEMALAN SAYING

IT TAKES A LONG TIME

People like you and I, though mortal of course like everyone else, do not grow old no matter how long we live. We never cease to stand like curious children before the great mystery into which we were born.

ALBERT EINSTEIN

If the angel deigns to come, it will be because you have convinced him, not by tears, but by your humble resolve to be always beginning: to be a beginner.

RAINER MARIA RILKE

The world is round and the place which may seem like the end may also be only the beginning.

MARY STUART

Every child is an artist. The problem is how to remain an artist once she grows up.

PABLO PICASSO

The creation of something new is not accomplished by the intellect but by the play instinct acting from inner necessity. The creative mind plays with the objects it loves.

C.G. JUNG

The great man is he who does not lose his childlike heart.

MENCIUS

TO BECOME YOUNG